D1529112

6/14 Kim

OLIGARCHY

LEEANNE GELLETLY

MASON CREST
PHILADELPHIA

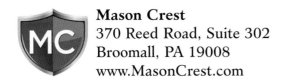

Mason Crest
370 Reed Road, Suite 302
Broomall, PA 19008
www.MasonCrest.com

Printed and bound in the United States of America

CPSIA Compliance Information: Batch #MEG2012-7. For further information, contact Mason Crest at 1-866-MCP-Book.

First printing
1 3 5 7 9 8 6 4 2

Library of Congress Cataloging-in-Publication Data

Gelletly, LeeAnne.
   Oligarchy / LeeAnne Gelletly.
         p. cm. — (Major forms of world government)
   Includes bibliographical references and index.
   ISBN 978-1-4222-2142-6 (hc)
   ISBN 978-1-4222-9459-8 (ebook)
   1.   Oligarchy—Juvenile literature.   I. Title.
   JC419.G45 2013
   321'.5—dc23
                           2012027858

Publisher's note: All quotations in this book are taken from original sources, and contain the spelling and grammatical inconsistencies of the original texts.

TITLES IN THIS SERIES

COMMUNISM	MILESTONES	MONARCHY
DEMOCRACY	IN THE EVOLUTION	OLIGARCHY
DICTATORSHIP	OF GOVERNMENT	THEOCRACY
FASCISM		

TABLE OF CONTENTS

INTRODUCTION by Dr. Timothy Colton, Harvard University

When human beings try to understand complex sets of things, they usually begin by sorting them into categories. They classify or group the phenomena that interest them into boxes that are basically very much alike. These boxes can then be compared and analyzed. The logic of classification applies to the study of inanimate objects (such as, for example, bodies of water or minerals), to living organisms (such as species of birds or bacteria), and also to man-made systems (such as religions or communications media).

This series of short books is about systems of government, which are specific and very important kinds of man-made systems. Systems of government are arrangements for human control and cooperation on particular territories. Governments dispense justice, make laws, raise taxes, fight wars, run school and health systems, and perform many other services that we often take for granted. Like, say, minerals, bacteria, and religions, systems of government come in a wide variety of forms or categories.

Just what are those categories? One of the earliest attempts to answer this question rigorously was made in the fourth century BCE by the brilliant Greek philosopher Aristotle. His study *Politics* has come down to us in incomplete form, as many of his writings were lost after he died. Nonetheless, it contains a simple and powerful scheme for classifying systems of government. Aristotle researched and illustrated his treatise by looking at the constitutions of 158 small city-states near the eastern shores of the Mediterranean Sea of his day, most of them inhabited by Greeks.

According to Aristotle's *Politics*, any system of government could be accurately classified and thus understood once two things were known. The first was, how many people were involved in making political decisions: one person, a small number, or a large number. The second issue was whether the system was designed to serve the common good of the citizens of the city-state. Taken together, these distinctions produced six categories of governmental system in all: monarchy (rule by one civic-minded person); tyranny (rule by one selfish person); aristocracy (rule by the few in the interests of all); oligarchy (rule by the few to suit themselves); constitutional government or "polity" (rule by the many in the common interest); and finally a form of mob rule (rule by the many with no concern for the greater good).

The fifth of these classic categories comes closest to modern representative democracy, as it is experienced in the United States, Western Europe, India, and many other places. One of the things Aristotle teaches us, however, is that there are many alternatives to this setup. In addition to the volume on democracy, this Mason Crest series will acquaint students with systems of government that correspond in rough terms to other categories invented by Aristotle more than two thousand years ago. These include monarchy; dictatorship (in Aristotle's terms, tyranny); oligarchy; communism (which we might think of as a particular kind of modern-day oligarchy); fascism (which combines some of the characteristics of tyranny and mob rule); and theocracy (which does not fit easily into Aristotle's scheme, although we might think of it as tyranny or oligarchy, but in the name of some divine being or creed).

Aristotle focused his research on the written constitutions of city-states. Today, political scientists, with better tools at their disposal, delve more into the actual practice of government in different countries. That practice frequently differs from the theory written into the constitution. Scholars study why it is that countries differ so much in terms of how and in whose interests governmental decisions are taken, across broad categories and within these categories, as well as in mixed systems that cross the boundaries between categories. It turns out that there are not one but many reasons for these differences, and there are significant disagreements about which reasons are most important. Some of the reasons are examined in this book series.

Experts on government also wonder a lot about trends over time. Why is it that some version of democracy has come to be the most common form of government in the contemporary world? Why has democratization come in distinct waves, with long periods of stagnation or even of reverse de-democratization separating them? The so-called third wave of democratization began in the 1970s and extended into the 1990s, and featured, among other changes, the collapse of communist systems in the Soviet Union and Eastern Europe and the disintegration of differently constituted nondemocratic systems in Southern Europe and Latin America. At the present time, the outlook for democracy is uncertain. In a number of Arab countries, authoritarian systems of government have recently been overthrown or challenged by revolts. And yet, it is far from clear that the result will be functioning democracies. Moreover, it is far from clear that the world will not encounter another wave of de-democratization. Nor can we rule out the rise of fundamentally new forms of government not foreseen by Aristotle; these might be encouraged by contemporary forms of technology and communication, such as the Internet, behavioral tracking devices, and social media.

For young readers to be equipped to consider complex questions like these, they need to begin with the basics about existing and historical systems of government. It is to meet their educational needs that this book series is aimed.

A group of people hold protest signs at the Occupy Wall Street demonstration in Zuccotti Park near the New York Stock Exchange, September 2011.

OLIGARCHY AND THE ELITE

On Saturday, September 17, 2011, hundreds of protesters gathered in Zuccotti Park, in the financial district of New York City. Calling their demonstration "Occupy Wall Street," the protesters set up tents. (Wall Street is the site of many U.S. banking and investment institutions.) The demonstrators announced they would stay until their demands were addressed. Referring to themselves as "the 99 percent," the occupiers claimed that the "wealthiest 1 percent" of people in the country and their corporations had too much influence on the U.S. government and its policies. The U.S. government was being run by a financial oligarchy, they said, and it had to change.

WHAT IS AN OLIGARCHY?

An oligarchy is a form of government in which a small privileged group rules or holds political power, typically for corrupt or selfish purposes. The term comes from the Greek words *oligoi*, meaning "a few," and *arkhein*, "to rule." Oligarchies may govern societies or organizations.

Not all oligarchs are rich. Sometimes they are simply members of a privileged group that holds power. They may be born into royalty or an upper class. Or they may have family, corporate, or military connections. In some cases, oligarchies consist of members of a particular ethnic group or race. But even if not rich, oligarchs have access to political and economic benefits that enable them to become wealthy.

SOCIAL CLASS

The ancient Greeks were the first to describe oligarchy as a form of government. For the Greek philosopher Aristotle (384 BC–322 BC), the crucial elements distinguishing different forms of government were how many people held power (one, a few, or many), and whether they ruled for the public good or for their own selfish purposes. Oligarchy, Aristotle said, was rule by a few for their own benefit.

In his long essay *Politics*, the Greek philosopher Aristotle described different types of government systems found in the ancient world, including oligarchy.

Aristotle also recognized the influence of social class on government. He wrote that oligarchy, which was a common form of government in Greece during his time, was rule by the rich, or upper class. By contrast, democracy—which Aristotle equated with mob rule—resulted when the poor, or lower class, held political power.

Aristotle argued that an ideal form of government is one in which there is a large middle class in charge. In *Politics*, his great work on political philosophy, Aristotle wrote, "Great then is the good fortune of a state in which the citizens have a moderate and sufficient property; for where some possess much, and the others nothing, there may arise an extreme democracy, or a pure oligarchy." In either case, the rich and poor would have completely different goals. By contrast, in societies where the majority of people have moderate wealth, Aristotle believed, citizens would be more likely to work together. "[W]here the middle class is large," he wrote, "there are least likely to be factions and dissensions."

> "DEMOCRATS SAY THAT JUSTICE IS THAT TO WHICH THE MAJORITY AGREE, OLIGARCHS THAT TO WHICH THE WEALTHIER CLASS [AGREE]."
>
> —ARISTOTLE

UPPER AND LOWER CLASSES

Extreme differences in class status, education, and income often exist in societies with oligarchy. The ruling upper class holds the privileges that come with political and economic power. They have easy access to the best education, legal protection, and healthcare. And their influence gives them access to resources and information needed to amass even greater wealth and power.

In some oligarchic systems, most people in the lower class are extremely poor and uneducated. They have almost no influence in government. And, when the oligarchy is autocratic—meaning it doesn't tolerate any political opposition—members of the lower class have few options to improve their situation. Under these circumstances, conflict between the "haves" and "have-nots" may lead oppressed people to try to overthrow the government through revolution. Because of the potential for class conflict in oligarchy, many political theorists consider it an unstable form of government.

ELECTED AND HEREDITARY OLIGARCHIES

Aristotle wrote about various kinds of oligarchies that existed in ancient Greece. In elected oligarchies, citizens elected the ruling members to

In the United States, some wealthy businesspeople have used their personal fortunes to finance their own campaigns for public office. For example, billionaire Michael Bloomberg, one of the wealthiest people in the United States, spent over $150 million on his three successful campaigns for mayor of New York City.

government positions. However, not everyone could run for office. For example, in some oligarchic governments, candidates could run for office only if they were born into a ruling family or owned a specified amount of land.

Another kind of system was a hereditary oligarchy. Under this system, the members of the ruling oligarchy came only from politically powerful families. Political power was passed on to the son upon the death of the father. Aristotle noted that in hereditary oligarchies powerful ruling families typically held absolute power.

THE ELITE

Other political thinkers have theorized about oligarchy. The German-born sociologist Robert Michels (1876–1936) defined oligarchy as elitism—that is, governing in the hands of the elite. "The elite" can be defined as a small number of people who have significant influence over

> # KEY IDEA
>
> Defined as "rule by a few," oligarchy is commonly viewed as rule by the extremely rich. Oligarchs may head governments or use their political power to shape public policy for the benefit of themselves or their group.

social and political change. Such power may be based on their wealth, their access to institutions of power, or their ability to persuade. The elite typically exercise power in the interest of their own class.

Michels proposed a political theory known as the "iron law of oligarchy." It states that all organizations eventually concentrate authority in the hands of a few in order to operate efficiently. This rule applies everywhere—including social organizations, political parties, and trade unions. "Who says organization, says oligarchy," Michels explained in his book *Political Parties: A Sociological Study of the Oligarchical Tendencies of Modern Democracy*. According to Michels, all governing systems eventually become oligarchies.

DEFENDING WEALTH

Northwestern University professor Jeffrey Winters says that Michels's iron law describes elitism, but not necessarily oligarchy. In his book *Oligarchy* (2011), Winters accepts the definition of oligarchy as rule by the few. But the few hold an extreme concentration of wealth. Defending this wealth, which is an important power resource, is the main objective of oligarchs, he argues. "The common thread for all oligarchs across history is that wealth defines them, empowers them, and inherently exposes them to a range of threats," Winters writes. "What varies across history is the nature of the threats and how oligarchs respond to defend their wealth."

Winters describes four kinds of oligarchies. In *warring oligarchies*, armed autocratic rulers use coercion and violence when other oligarchs threaten their power. An example would be the feudal barons of medieval Europe.

In *ruling oligarchies*, oligarchs govern collectively and rule directly through governmental institutions. Such forms of government existed in ancient Greece and Rome, as well as in Italian city-states during the late medieval and early Renaissance periods.

Winters also describes *sultanistic oligarchies*, in which power is in the hands of a lead oligarch who holds final authority, and who is not restricted by any laws, especially regarding property rights. This leader exercises power by control of the armed forces, police, and security forces. Winters describes the Indonesian government during the rule of Suharto (1968–1998) as a sultanistic oligarchy.

In *civil oligarchies*, the ruling group does not govern directly, although it has power behind the scenes. Civil oligarchies can exist only in countries where laws strongly protect property rights. Civil oligarchs use political power, rather than violence, to ensure that the laws reflect their own interests. In his book, Winters identifies the United States as an example of a civil oligarchy.

This claim is quite controversial. Most political scientists view the United States today as a flawed representative democracy, whose political system has become overly responsive to the interests of the very wealthy. For his part, Winters doesn't regard democracy and oligarchy as mutually exclusive. "To argue that the United States is a thriving oligarchy," he writes, "does not imply that our democracy is a sham: There are many policies about which oligarchs have no shared interests. Their influence in these areas is either small or mutually canceling."

2

OLIGARCHIES IN THE CLASSICAL WORLD

ncient Greece, where oligarchy was first described, was not a unified nation. Rather, it was a collection of city-states that shared a common language and culture. These city-states began to emerge around the ninth century BC, as neighboring villages with trade ties joined together to form larger communities.

Called a *polis* (plural: *poleis*), the Greek city-state was governed by the citizens living in and around the urban center. They worked together in running its institutions. The English word *politics* comes from *polis*.

OLIGARCHIES AND TYRANNIES

Early Greek city-states were ruled by kings, whose family members inherited the throne. But by the eighth century BC, most monarchies had been replaced by oligarchies.

The Greek city-state of Athens is considered the birthplace of democratic government. However, at many times in the ancient city-state's history, wealthy landowning oligarchs ruled Athens.

In the Greek oligarchies, the *eupatridae*, or wellborn, controlled the best land and the greatest amount of land. This made them rich. These wealthiest citizens shared the absolute authority of a monarch. What gave them claim to power was not noble birth, however, but the fact they held greater wealth than others in the community. In some Greek city-states the oligarchy elected an *archon*, or chief magistrate (government official), to head the government.

In many cases, an individual overthrew the oligarchy and seized power by mobilizing support from the lower classes, or from a particular faction. Such a usurper—often a former member of the oligarchy—was known as a tyrant. Today the term refers to a cruel and repressive ruler. In ancient Greece, however, the word *tyrant* referred simply to someone who had seized power without legal right. Some Greek tyrants apparently were quite popular.

To fend off challenges to their power, tyrants had to be able to bring to bear some degree of force. In certain cases a group of bodyguards was sufficient. In other cases tyrants commanded a larger army. Some tyrants attempted to establish hereditary monarchies. However, most tyrannies were unstable, and tyrants were frequently overthrown.

MAJOR CITY-STATES

By the sixth century BC, there were about 1,500 separate Greek city-states located around the shores of the Mediterranean, Aegean, and Black Seas. The largest were in today's southern Greece. They included Argos, Athens, Corinth, Mycenae, Sparta, and Thebes. Other major city-states in 500 BC were Ephesus and Miletus, in modern-day Turkey, and Knossos, on the island of Crete.

The people in the Greek city-states called themselves Hellenes and their land Hellas. Although Greeks shared the same culture, religion, and language (albeit with regional dialects), their governments operated independently of one another. And they frequently clashed.

DEMOCRACY IN ATHENS

One of the richest and most powerful Greek city-states was Athens. During the seventh century BC, its monarchy was abolished and an oligarchy established. At that time, Athens was governed by a board of

In the oligarchic governments of ancient Greece, the common people played only a limited role in government. Major political offices were held mostly by members of the aristocracy and the very wealthy.

nine archons, all of whom were members of the nobility. Archons served one-year terms, after which they became lifetime members of the Council of the Areopagus. It was composed of men of the noble class. The Areopagus held the power to judge legal cases, and it selected the new archons each year. In this manner, the Athenian nobility kept a firm hold on the reins of power.

But reforms introduced in the early sixth century BC changed the nature of the Athenian oligarchy. For the first time, wealth rather than noble birth alone was made the criterion for membership in the Areopagus. In addition, an assembly of ordinary Athenian citizens was given a voice in picking archons.

These reforms, along with other developments in Athens, helped shift political power away from the elite. By 500 BC the Athenian oligarchy had been replaced with a new form of government: democracy. In Athens all adult male citizens, regardless of social station, had the right to vote directly on proposed laws in an assembly. They were also eligible to hold a variety of government offices. It should be noted, however, that the Athenian democracy excluded from participation all women, slaves, and foreign-born people living in the city.

Still, the achievements of citizen self-government in Athens were significant. Other Greek city-states followed the Athenian example, setting up democratic governments as well. But tyrants and oligarchies continued to rule many other city-states.

> "IN ALL AGES, WHATEVER THE FORM AND NAME OF GOVERNMENT, BE IT MONARCHY, REPUBLIC, OR DEMOCRACY, AN OLIGARCHY LURKS BEHIND THE FAÇADE."
>
> —OXFORD PROFESSOR AND HISTORIAN RONALD SYME

OLIGARCHY IN SPARTA

The city-state of Sparta, located in the southeastern Peloponnesus peninsula, had a powerful and entrenched oligarchy. It was based in Sparta's highly militaristic society.

Males who were full citizens of Sparta,

In Sparta, a small group of elites controlled the government. The Spartan oligarchy was dedicated to maintaining the city-state's strong military position.

known as *Spartiates*, spent almost their entire lives preparing for and fighting in wars. They didn't do manual labor and were forbidden to engage in any commercial activity. At the age of seven, Spartiate boys were removed from their families to undergo years of often-brutal military training. Those who completed this training became members of the Spartan army at age 20, and full citizens 10 years later. At that point, they were permitted to marry, though they had to continue living in barracks and could visit their wives only infrequently.

Each Spartiate received land and subjugated people known as *helots* to farm it. *Helots*, who made up the great majority of the population in areas controlled by Sparta, were bound to the land like serfs. But they were subject to random violence at the hands of their Spartiate masters. In fact, the training of elite Spartan soldiers included sneaking into the countryside and murdering helots.

The government of the Roman Republic was not the same as republics today. In the modern world, a republic is defined as a representative democracy. It is a government in which people hold power through elected representatives and an elected head of government.

Spartan society also included a class of merchants and artisans known as *perioikoi*. Though free, they weren't citizens.

Sparta's government was headed by two kings. They led the army and served, along with 28 Spartiates aged 60 or older, in a council called the Gerousia. Its members served for life. The Gerousia presented proposals to Sparta's assembly, the Apella. The Apella, which was open to all Spartiates age 30 or older, elected new members of the Gerousia. Each year, the assembly also chose five magistrates known as *ephors*. They supervised the conduct of citizens and oversaw the education of Spartiate youths.

Sparta's governmental system was designed to keep power in the hands of the Spartiate oligarchy, which made up only about 10 percent of the population. Ultimately, though, it was the fearsome Spartan army that sustained the oligarchy.

PELOPONNESIAN WAR

In 431 BC Athens and Sparta, along with their respective allies, went to war. The conflict, known as the Peloponnesian War, lasted for 27 years.

In 411 BC, with the war going badly for Athens, the Athenian democracy was overthrown and oligarchs took control of the government. But the oligarchs were unable to hold power. Within a few months, democracy had been restored to Athens.

The Peloponnesian War finally ended in 404 BC. The victorious Spartans set up oligarchic rule in the lands they had conquered. But again, Athenians chafed under oligarchy. They soon reestablished democratic rule.

Sparta remained a powerful city-state until 371 BC, when it was conquered by a former ally, Thebes. Located north of Athens, Thebes was also ruled by an oligarchy. After defeating Sparta, it became the region's greatest military power.

Philip II, the king of neighboring Macedonia, would invade and conquer all of Greece. That conquest was completed in 338 BC. In the second century BC, Greece would come under the control of another military power: Rome.

THE ROMAN REPUBLIC

Rome, located in today's central Italy, had a republican form of government for about 500 years, from the late sixth century BC to the late first century BC. The Roman Republic featured elements of monarchy, aristocracy, and democracy.

In the Roman Republic, the motto SPQR represented an abbreviation of the Latin phrase *Senatus Populusque Romanus*, meaning "The Senate and the People of Rome." The inscription indicated that Roman citizens held political power in the republic. However, the Roman Senate, which gave a small group of elites the authority to rule Rome, was effectively an oligarchy.

The Roman government had an executive branch (similar to a monarchy), consisting of two annually elected chief magistrates known as *consuls*. The two consuls also commanded the army.

The aristocracy, made up of the landowning class called the *patricians*, dominated the Roman Senate, which approved government actions and policies. Many members of this group were extremely wealthy and owned huge estates. The Senate was composed of around 300 men elected for life to major government offices.

As in a democracy, there were also popular assemblies in which citizens voted and passed laws. In addition, they elected magistrates and the popular *tribunes* (officials who had veto powers over the Senate). The Century Assembly, made up of Roman soldiers, was responsible for electing the highest-ranking officials, including the consul. Both patricians and *plebeians* belonged to the Tribal Assembly, whose members elected citizens to less important political offices. Plebeians, or plebs, were the lower class of Roman citizens who were not aristocratic or wealthy. They included craftspeople, merchants, and small farmers.

The plebs had no political rights until the early fifth century BC, when the Plebeian Council was formed. Only plebeians belonged to this assembly, which at first passed laws that affected only members of the plebeian class. But the Plebian Council later gained more powers. It elected a tribune who could veto acts of the assemblies and of the Senate. After 287 BC any acts the Plebeian Council passed applied to both the Senate and people of Rome.

> The Roman Republic was an elective oligarchy in which only the wealthiest citizens held office. During the second century BC, ongoing conflict between the oligarchy and the plebeians brought about civil unrest that weakened the republic.

ROMAN OLIGARCHY

The role of the Senate evolved from providing advice to the consuls to direct governing as force of law. During the final century of the Roman Republic, known as the Late

In the second century BC, the Roman general and statesman Gaius Marius attempted to reduce the power of the oligarchs in the Senate and give greater power to the plebs, the Roman middle classes.

Republic, the Senate held much governing power. It oversaw wars and controlled foreign policy and day-to-day domestic policy.

Within the Senate an oligarchy of powerful families influenced policies and political offices. They were of patrician and plebeian classes. And they frequently held the most important political offices. From 233 to 133 BC, more than half of the consuls came from just 10 families. This elite group ran the Roman Republic in their own interest.

THE LATE REPUBLIC

Political turmoil characterized the Roman government during the Late Republic (147–30 BC). During that time plebeians struggled for equal rights with patricians. And the senatorial oligarchy worked to keep its privileges and power intact.

A few members of the oligarchy supported the common people. They gained great influence in the people's assemblies, especially in the Plebeian Council. One powerful supporter of plebeian rights was the Roman consul Gaius Marius (157–86 BC). In 107 the Plebeian Council voted to give him command of the Roman army in Africa. This was counter to tradition. Until then the Senate had the authority to run wars. After successfully ending the war in Africa, Marius headed Roman armies in battles against the Celtic tribes in Gaul (present-day France, Belgium, and Luxembourg). He also served as consul for five consecutive years, from 104 to 100.

Marius made reforms in the army. One significant change was allowing its members to include men who were not landowners. Before that time, landownership was a requirement for being a soldier. And most soldiers had been farmers who owned small plots. But as Rome engaged in distant wars, many soldiers had to sell their farms because they were not at home to work them. Marius's new system of military recruitment allowed men to become soldiers even if they did not possess property. This new class of soldiers had greater loyalty to their military commanders than to the Senate.

The transfer of the military's allegiance from the Senate to generals gave ambitious leaders the ability to use armies to gain power. During the first century BC, the Roman Republic saw numerous civil wars, mob violence, and assassinations. Historians date the end of the Roman Republic to 27 BC, with the establishment of a powerful monarchical form of government headed by the emperor Augustus Caesar. After 500 years in existence, the Roman Republic was replaced by the Roman Empire.

3

ITALIAN AND DUTCH REPUBLICS

For about a millennium after the fall of the Roman Empire in the late fifth century AD, monarchs ruled across much of Europe. The size of their realms varied considerably. By 1200, for example, all of England was united under the rule of the Plantagenet royal house. By contrast, the northern portion of what is today Spain consisted of a handful of Spanish Christian kingdoms, while the south (known as Al-Andalus) was controlled by the Muslim Almohad dynasty.

The Italian peninsula was not unified. The Kingdom of Sicily comprised the island of Sicily as well as the southern portion of the Italian peninsula. The Catholic Church, led by the pope, claimed the Papal States, located in the central part of the peninsula. But much of the rest of modern-day Italy consisted of independent city-states.

ITALY'S GUILD COMMUNES

Many urban centers of central and northern Italy were established as small, independent "communes." Prominent citizens, typically members of the nobility, were elected to govern for terms of two to three months. The ruler was assisted by a "Great Council," composed of members of the aristocracy. Through various representative citizen councils, the city-states created laws, maintained social order, and levied taxes. Councils also managed the defense of the city-state in times of war. Women, the clergy, and the working classes were excluded from participation in councils.

Another form of government coexisted with rule by the elite. Within the communes major professions were organized into guilds. These were self-governing associations with written statutes and executive and legislative bodies. The guilds were based on various trades. There were artisan, merchant, and many other kinds of guilds. Their members were not necessarily wealthy or of elite families, but they were literate, educated, and politically informed. Known as the *popolo*, they formed the middle ranks of Italian urban society. The *popolo* gathered in assemblies and voted on financial and other matters, including taxation.

During the late Middle Ages, associations of craftsmen known as guilds began to develop. The guilds exerted a strong influence over the economies and governments of communities in Italy, Germany, England, and other areas of Europe. This is the entrance to a guildhall in Perugia, a city in central Italy.

Within the guild system itself, there were major guilds, the *arti maggiori*, and minor guilds, the *arti minori*. Members of the major guilds included bankers, traders, and manufacturers. They, along with other influential professionals, made up the *popolo grasso*. By the 1300s this group had gained a share of economic, political, and military power previously held by the elite.

SIGNORIES AND OLIGARCHY

At the same time, some communal governments had given way to despotism. All civil and military power was in the hands of one dictatorial ruler—the *signor*. Some *signories* legitimized their power by purchasing titles from the Holy Roman Emperor, whose realm included modern-day Germany and northern Italy. For example, the Visconti family acquired the title of hereditary dukes of the city-state of Milan. The d'Este family became dukes of the city-state of Ferrara.

Other city-states became republics dominated by oligarchies. The ruling class included both members of the nobility and wealthy bankers and merchants—the *popolo grasso*. In several city-states the political elite formed a governing authority that was referred to as a *signoria*.

To maintain their exclusive claim to power, the ruling classes passed laws to control who was eligible for political office. In Venice and Florence, for example, those claiming noble status had to follow

During the 14th and 15th centuries many families of Italy's city-state oligarchies commissioned or sponsored works by Renaissance artists. As patrons of the arts, they funded the creation of many masterpieces in sculpture, painting, and architecture. At the same time the members of the upper class emphasized their own wealth and prestige. The elite helped turn their city-states into centers of the Renaissance cultural movement. Of particular importance were Florence, Milan, Venice, and Rome.

detailed official procedures in documenting their father and mother. A person's place in society was determined by his or her parents' place in society.

Among the independent city-states governed as oligarchic republics were Bologna, Genoa, Padua, and Siena. In each of these cities a few wealthy families rose to power and maintained authority for generations. But two of the most powerful republics under the control of oligarchies were Venice and Florence.

VENICE

Located in today's northeast Italy, along the Mediterranean Sea, Venice became a great trading center around the 1300s. It dominated commerce on the Mediterranean. Venice also had an aristocracy in which wealthy

This palace was the residence of the Doge of Venice, the leader of that Italian city-state's oligarchy from about AD 900 until 1797.

patrician families dominated. The republic was governed by an oligarchy of merchant-aristocrats.

The city-state had a *signoria* consisting of the chief magistrate, or Doge; a six-member Minor Council; and a three-member Supreme Tribunal. With the Minor Council and the Supreme Tribunal, the Doge of Venice served as leader of the republic. He ruled for life, after being elected in a complex process by members of the Great Council.

Only the aristocracy could belong to the Great Council, which had hundreds of members. All came from families whose names were published in the Venetian *Golden Book of the Nobility*. To be a member of the Great Council or hold any executive offices in Venice, one's name had to be on the list. Published in 1315, the book listed the most influential families in the city. It remained mostly unchanged for 200 years.

"IN THE CASE OF OCCUPIED STATES THAT HAVE BEEN USED TO LIVING WITH THEIR OWN LAWS IN LIBERTY, THERE ARE THREE MODES OF HOLDING THEM: FIRST, TO RUIN THEM; SECOND, GO LIVE PERSONALLY IN THEM; THIRD, LET THEM LIVE ACCORDING TO THEIR OWN LAWS, WHILE EXTRACTING TRIBUTE AND CREATING A FAITHFUL OLIGARCHY THAT WILL KEEP THE STATE FRIENDLY."

—FROM *THE PRINCE*, BY ITALIAN PHILOSOPHER NICCOLÒ MACHIAVELLI

The most powerful group of oligarchs in Venice was the Council of Ten. This elite body, whose members came from the Great Council, operated in secret. Just 10 men held authority over all government acts and policies. And its members worked to prevent anyone from attempting to seize power in Venice and establish a monarchy.

FLORENCE

Located in the Tuscany region of central Italy, Florence was governed mostly by guild members during the early 1300s. There were many restrictions on eligibility to run for important political offices. In 1343 Florence had a population of around 80,000 people. But only 3,500 men were qualified to hold high office.

Electoral procedures were changed in 1400 so that only the traditional ruling families held or controlled the most powerful offices. Florence became an oligarchy in which about a dozen wealthy families dominated the government. The names of about 100 families, of both noble and merchant background, were listed as citizens eligible for other offices.

In the 15th century Florence gained importance as a banking center. This was due, in part, to one of its most prominent families—the Medicis. Its members founded the Medici Bank, which became the largest financial

Although he never held public office, Cosimo de' Medici used his wealth in order to control the government of Florence in the 15th century. The Medici family exerted influence over government affairs in Florence for several generations.

institution in Europe. It had branches in the major Italian city-states of Rome, Milan, and Venice. Medici banks could also be found in Avignon, France; in Bruges, in the Burgundian Netherlands; and in London, England. The Medicis had controlling interests in Florence's wool and silk industries and in the mining of alum, which was used to dye textiles.

By 1434 Cosimo de' Medici had created an oligarchy in Florence that benefited the members of his extended family. He maintained power behind the scenes, by manipulating elections, finances, foreign policy, and political institutions. After his death in 1464, the Medicis remained in power for another 30 years. However, none of them held title or office. A grandson, Lorenzo de' Medici, held leadership from 1469 until his death in 1492. He is credited with supporting the Renaissance culture that flourished in Florence during the late 1400s.

In 1494 the armies of Charles VII of France invaded Italy. The French expelled the Medicis from Florence. But with help from Spain, the other Italian city-states fought back. For three decades, French and Spanish forces fought for control of the lands of Italy. Spain finally prevailed in 1527.

DUTCH REPUBLIC

Less than a century later, an oligarchic government established power in northern Europe. The Dutch Republic came into being in 1581 when the Dutch Low Countries (today's Netherlands, Belgium, and Luxembourg) signed a formal declaration of independence from Spain. The nation was also known as the Republic of the Seven United Netherlands.

The Dutch Republic was a confederation of provinces. And each province was independent and self-governing. The towns within the provinces were also governed independently. Among the most powerful provinces were Friesland, Gelderland, Holland, and Zeeland.

A TRADE ECONOMY

In the 1600s Dutch ships traveled around the world. Through the Dutch East India Company, founded in 1602, and the Dutch West India Company, established in 1621, merchants controlled a vast commercial empire. And they amassed great fortunes. Dutch trading posts and colonies provided various goods. Silk, spices, and teas came from the Cape of Good Hope, in today's South Africa; Ceylon, in modern-day Sri Lanka; and Malacca, in today's Malaysia. Sugar was shipped from Dutch colonies in South America, including Guiana and Dutch Brazil.

The Dutch also developed a powerful banking industry. Its biggest financial institution was the Bank of Amsterdam, founded in 1609. It eventually became the chief bank of Europe.

Wealthy merchants helped make the Netherlands a world power in the 17th century. In 1602 the merchants formed the Dutch East India Company, which was granted the power to establish and govern overseas colonies in Asia. The company was extremely profitable for nearly 200 years.

The profitable trade ensured that the Dutch Republic was economically and socially stable. The sciences and arts flourished. And the mid-17th century became known as the Dutch Golden Age.

MERCHANT OLIGARCHIES

The Dutch cities, provinces, and the republic itself were controlled by a small ruling class. Some of its members were of the aristocracy. However, most ruling members came from the merchant class.

The merchant oligarchies had the greatest economic power in the province of Holland and the city of Amsterdam. Holland was the richest of all the provinces in the Dutch Republic. A majority of the province's wealth came from Amsterdam. The seaport city was both the center of the shipping trade and a leading financial center.

The Maluku Islands of Indonesia, also known as the Spice Islands, were largely controlled by the Dutch in the 1600s. In its trade with Maluku, the Dutch East India Company dealt with an oligarchy of *orangkaya*, or merchant-aristocrats, in the Banda Islands. But in 1621 the Dutch took direct control. The Dutch East India Company overthrew the government and turned Banda into a company-owned estate worked by slaves.

Wealthy Dutch merchant families typically dominated the top government posts. These ruling officials, called *regents*, often held their positions for life. In city government, these regents served as sheriffs, burgomasters (chief magistrates), aldermen, or members of the city council (*vroedschap*).

The ordinary citizen had no voice in government. City regents governed all local aspects of life. In Amsterdam men could join the ruling class only if they met certain requirements. They needed a specified amount of wealth. And they had to live a required number of years as a resident in the city. Family ties were also important. Aspiring regents would arrange to marry into families whose members already held government offices.

While oligarchs ruled the Netherlands, Amsterdam became a major financial center in Europe. It also was home to the first full-time stock exchange (the Borse, pictured here in the late 19th century).

Amsterdam's merchant oligarchy also had great influence in Holland. Each province handled its own local and domestic matters through a governing body called the Estates. This group was made up of delegates from the province's towns and rural areas. The Estates of Holland, for example, was made up of delegates from the province's 18 major towns. (Delegates to the Estates were chosen from among town regents.) The Estates of Holland also included some landholding nobles from rural areas. Each city had veto power. But the city of Amsterdam held great influence in the Estates because it contributed a significant amount of Holland's annual budget.

In addition to controlling the provincial government, the Amsterdam merchant oligarchy also influenced the States-General. This was the Dutch Republic's central form of government. It consisted of representatives from each of the seven provinces. Each provincial deputation had a single vote. But Amsterdam frequently asserted its sovereignty by overriding decisions of the majority.

The States-General had no authority to force provinces to go along with its decisions and policies. And its members did not hold power in the affairs of provinces. That power belonged to the Estates.

Several factors gave the Amsterdam oligarchy a leading role in the States-General. The organization's meetings were held in Holland. The States-General met at The Hague, the capital of the province. In addition, Holland contributed about 60 percent of the States-General's annual budget. The province's economic influence gave it a strong voice in the Dutch Republic's foreign policy, tax collection, and navy.

The Dutch Republic remained a European power for two centuries. But internal political unrest and war with England during the second half of the 18th century weakened it. In 1795 the Dutch Republic fell to France, which established the Batavian Republic in its place.

Native American slaves cultivate sugarcane on a Spanish plantation in the Caribbean, 17th century. The multi-level social system established by the conquistadors in Central and South America would eventually result in the emergence of governments dominated by rich landowners.

4

COLONIAL RULE AND OLIGARCHIES

During the 1500s several European powers, in addition to the Dutch, funded the journeys of explorers. Motivated by the possibility of finding riches in new lands, the Spanish and Portuguese governments gave financial backing to numerous seafaring expeditions. Between the 1500s and 1800s they would claim large portions of land in the "New World" of the Americas. And Spain and Portugal would greatly increase their empires.

SPANISH AND PORTUGUESE COLONIZATION

In the 1500s Spanish-backed explorers Hernán Cortés and Francisco Pizarro were among the most successful conquerors, or *conquistadors*, of the New World. The Spanish took power in most

35

of South America, Central America, and parts of North America, including today's Mexico. The Spanish Empire ultimately ran from today's California and Mexico to modern-day Argentina. The Portuguese asserted ownership over much of modern-day Brazil.

The indigenous people of the Americas did not view land as private property that could be owned by individuals. But the Europeans did. The Spanish crown considered the conquered lands as its own. And it granted large swaths of territory to conquistadors in reward for their military service. Cortés, for example, received lands encompassing much of today's Mexican state of Morelos.

Control of property virtually guaranteed riches. Some lands harbored mineral wealth—precious metals such as gold and silver or mineral deposits of copper and tin. Other property was fertile and well suited for farming. In the years that followed, plantation estates produced lucrative cash crops such as cacao, coffee, bananas, and sugar. Other large tracts of land became cattle ranches. (The Spanish introduced livestock to the New World.) The large landholdings of mines, plantations, and ranches were known as *haciendas* in Spanish-speaking America. In Brazil they were called by the Portuguese term *fazendas*.

Along with the land grants, the Spanish crown gave conquistadors "stewardship" of the indigenous people living on the land. Using military force, the new landowners exploited the native Americans as cheap labor. The local people were

SOUTH AFRICA

Colonial rule in South Africa led to the development of oligarchic rule based on race. The South African government instituted apartheid, or racial segregation, in 1948. Those with privilege and power were English- and Afrikaans-speaking whites of European descent. Under apartheid, which lasted until 1994, South Africa was ruled by a privileged group— a white oligarchy. Black Africans had few opportunities for education or jobs.

forced to toil in the mines and fields. Many of them died because of brutal treatment and disease.

SOCIAL HIERARCHY

In the centuries that followed under the colonial system, there was a stratified social structure. The upper class consisted of people of European heritage—those who owned or controlled the land. The owners of haciendas were referred to as *hacendados*. They had great wealth and political power.

This lower class was made up of the landless indigenous population and people of mixed race, called *mestizos*. Members of the rural lower class, called *campesinos*, provided cheap labor. And they typically lived in poverty.

Even after the colonial system collapsed in the early 1800s, the social hierarchy remained. As new nations were founded in Central and South America, the upper classes held on to power. In many countries, wealthy landowners played a part in organizing the government. They obtained high positions. And they strongly influenced political policies. Among the most powerful were those whose lands produced the country's major exports, such as coffee or bananas. At the end of the 1800s many nations of Central and South America were controlled by oligarchies. Those groups consisted of upper-class, predominantly white families.

MAINTAINING POWER

The extremes of wealth and poverty common to oligarchic rule frequently led to civil unrest. Activists tried to carry out agrarian reform. This refers to redistributing agricultural lands so that more members of society own property. But oligarchies in power blocked attempts at reform.

A major goal of an oligarchy is to protect property and maintain the status quo. In Latin America the elite families maintained firm control of the land and of the labor force. This was accomplished by forming political alliances with the military. When the poor protested their situation, armed forces put down any uprisings.

Historians have referred to the power balance that existed in Central and South America as a triumvirate of oligarchy, church, and armed forces.

Historically, oligarchs in South and Central America shared power with the Roman Catholic Church as well as with local military leaders.

The landowning elite frequently had to bargain and compromise with the Catholic Church, which also had large landholdings received from the Spanish crown. Oligarchs also bargained with the military to ensure its leaders would enforce their policies. Oligarchies were known to support military dictatorships because such governments provided political and economic stability.

At times, revolt by the lower classes against oligarchies helped the military take full political power. Armed forces would overthrow an oligarchy-dominated government in a coup d'etat. Such coups often led to rule by a dictator or a military junta. Between the 1930s and 1980s in Central and South America, dictators frequently assumed power. An exception was Costa Rica, which remained a democracy throughout much of the 20th century.

EXAMPLES OF OLIGARCHY IN CENTRAL AMERICA

In the early 1820s, what would eventually become the countries of Guatemala, El Salvador, Honduras, Nicaragua, and Costa Rica declared independence from Spain and Mexico and formed the United Provinces of Central America. Within two decades, hopes for a prosperous and democratic republic were dashed amid civil war. In the smaller independent states formed in the aftermath, prosperity didn't extend to the majority of people. Wealthy oligarchs dominated. The poor remained poor and were excluded from the political system.

EL SALVADOR: In the late 1800s, coffee became a major export of El Salvador. In fact, this cash crop formed the foundation of the country's

Pedestrians walk past the presidential palace in San Salvador, the capital of El Salvador, circa 1911. For decades the wealthy owners of coffee plantations dominated the government of this Central American country.

entire economy. And an oligarchy of landowning families controlled coffee production and the levers of political power. Members of *las catorce familias*, or the 14 families, dominated the presidency and legislative bodies. During the 19th century the oligarchy promoted the passage of laws that created huge coffee haciendas. The laws stated that most land had to be used to grow coffee. The military assisted by forcing small farmers and indigenous tribes off arable land.

When a military coup overthrew the government in 1931, the coffee oligarchy supported it. But the lower classes rebelled. They were brutally repressed. In 1932 at least 30,000 of them were massacred by the country's armed forces.

The oligarchy continued to hold economic and political power. Little was done to develop the country economically and improve the lot of campesinos. Government repression led to the formation, in 1980, of the left-leaning Farabundo Martí National Liberation Front (FMLN). This guerrilla group battled the right-wing government backed by the coffee oligarchs. A majority in the legislature was held by the Nationalist Republican Alliance (ARENA), the political party headed by Roberto D'Aubuisson. An officer in the Salvadoran army, D'Aubuisson was also accused of commanding "death squads" that abducted, tortured, and murdered thousands of civilians.

El Salvador's civil war raged for 12 years. By the end of the war the Salvadoran oligarchy had lost its power. However, some analysts insist that El Salvador still has elites who continue to compete against each other.

PANAMA. An oligarchy dominated politics in Panama after that country broke away (with U.S. encouragement) from the South American

> In many countries of Central and South America the colonial system of land distribution resulted in the rise of a wealthy few landowning families and the formation of oligarchies. Oligarchies became strong political forces in many of these countries after they became independent republics.

nation of Colombia in 1903. The following year Panama became a democratic republic with the adoption of a new constitution. From then until 1968, through its alliance with the Liberal Party (PLN), the Panamanian oligarchy controlled the nation's politics.

The oligarchy was made up of aristocratic families of Spanish descent and immigrants involved in the development of the Panama Canal. (The U.S.-built canal stretches across the Isthmus of Panama, connecting the Atlantic and Pacific Oceans.) Members of this often American-educated elite group provided presidents, cabinet ministers, and members of the legislature. The oligarchy controlled Panama until 1968, when President Arnulfo Arias Madrid was ousted in a coup.

EXAMPLES OF OLIGARCHY IN SOUTH AMERICA

Twelve independent nations make up the continent of South America. It has a geography ranging from vast grassy plains to high, rugged mountains. The largest country is Brazil.

BRAZIL: In the Portuguese-speaking country of Brazil, the first oligarchic families were wealthy coffee growers living in the southeastern states of São Paulo and Minas Gerais. Coffee was the country's biggest export, and the oligarchy had great economic influence. In São Paulo, it also wielded national political power. Its members traditionally held high offices, including the presidency. The São Paulo oligarchy provided the nation's first civilian president, Prudente de Morais (1894–98), and his successor, Manuel Ferraz de Campos Sales (1898–1902). Because of the power of the coffee growers, Brazil during the period 1894–1930 is often referred to as the *República das Oligarquias*, or Republic of the Oligarchies.

Members of local oligarchies held influence under the *coronelismo* system. This referred to the political rule of the local *coronel* (Portuguese for "colonel"), who was typically the largest landowner. The *coronel* controlled the votes of rural workers and their families, often through coercion or violence. In exchange for votes, politicians bestowed appointments on the local bosses or provided for local public works.

Brazil's coffee oligarchs lost most of their national influence after 1930. That year, the Brazilian republic fell to a dictatorship headed by Getúlio Vargas.

PERU: Peru gained full independence from Spain in 1824, although the Spanish government did not officially recognize the nation until 1879. For the next 15 years Peru suffered political turmoil as various governments rose and fell. The year 1895 saw the overthrow of a dictator and the establishment of the "Aristocratic Republic," headed by president Nicolás de Piérola. The elite, who owned haciendas in Peru's mountains and plantations on its coast, held direct rule. For the next several decades, the Peruvian oligarchy provided most of the republic's presidents.

The oligarchy—which was composed predominantly of whites—also took more land from the indigenous Quechua and Aymara peoples, who made up a majority of Peru's population. By the turn of the 20th century, the landed oligarchy was also basing its power and wealth on foreign investment in the country's industries.

Political turmoil returned to Peru around 1930, but through its alliance with the military, the oligarchy maintained power. The military suppressed rebellions by leftists, and the oligarchy continued to exclude the middle and lower classes from the political process. Then, in 1968, General Juan Velasco Alvarado seized power in a bloodless coup. As president he instituted agrarian reforms that brought the economic power of the oligarchy to an end.

ARGENTINA: A landed and commercial elite influenced the government in Argentina. In this nation, various factions representing different interests took power, but governing was always by the landowners. Around 300 families owned most of the land. They had large rural estates, or *estancias*, that each consisted of hundreds of thousands of acres of fertile land. In 1866 these families formed an elite group called the Argentine Rural Society. One of its members, Julio Roca, became president in 1880.

For the next 30 years subsequent presidents and political favor would be shared among the members of the Argentine Rural Society oligarchy. Its control over the state and politics fueled anger against the elite. And new political parties demanding reforms ultimately emerged. But it was not until the elections of 1916 that the oligarchy was removed from power.

SOUTH AMERICAN SOCIALISM

Dissatisfaction with governments ruled by wealthy oligarchs and corrupt dictators often led to changes in governments. In some cases they also led to the establishment of socialist-leaning governments in democracies. *Socialism* refers to a system in which there is shared or governmental ownership and regulation of the production and distribution of goods. Supporters of socialism consider oligarchic rule as a symbol of capitalism.

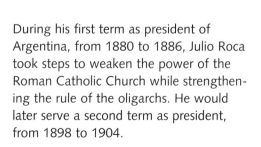

During his first term as president of Argentina, from 1880 to 1886, Julio Roca took steps to weaken the power of the Roman Catholic Church while strengthening the rule of the oligarchs. He would later serve a second term as president, from 1898 to 1904.

Capitalism is an economic system in which a country's trade and industry are controlled by private owners for profit, without intervention by the government. In the early 2000s several Central and South American republics elected leaders who promoted socialism.

BOLIVIA: Since gaining independence from Spain in 1825, Bolivia has been politically unstable, undergoing almost 200 coups in its history. A silver- and tin-mining elite held power from 1879 to 1932. At that time,

Since coming to power in Venezuela, Hugo Chávez has regularly claimed that his political opponents are part of an oligarchy that is working against him. He has privatized industries and redistributed land in order to weaken the power of wealthy Venezuelans, as well as to ensure that he remains in control of the state.

Bolivia was a republic but the native Quechua and Aymara did not have the right to vote. Only males who could speak, read, and write Spanish held that right.

After much upheaval, Bolivia was established as a democracy in 1982. In the 2005 elections a socialist leader, Evo Morales, became the first indigenous president of the country. He and the leader of Venezuela, Hugo Chávez, vehemently oppose the oligarchies as a product of capitalism.

VENEZUELA: President since 1999, Hugo Chávez often rails against oligarchies both inside and outside Venezuela. In 2004 he claimed to have rid the nation's courts, legislature, and press of the "rancid oligarchy." In February 2008 he accused the Colombian "oligarchy" and its government (which is backed by the United States) of making false accusations against his government. "From Colombia, Venezuela is threatened," he claimed. "The oligarchy attacks us."

Mexican businessman Carlos Slim Helú has used some of his vast fortune—estimated at more than $70 billion—to influence elections in Mexico and to ensure that the government helps his companies to profit.

5

FINANCIAL OLIGARCHS

In 2011 the world population approached 7 billion. Slightly over 1,200 of those people, according to *Forbes* magazine, were billionaires.

Having billions (or even hundreds of millions) of dollars doesn't necessarily make a person anything other than super-rich. But clearly some of the world's richest people—in countries as diverse as Russia and Mexico, China and the United States—have used their wealth to mold the political process for their own benefit. These people have, in other words, acted the part of oligarchs.

MEXICO

In July 2006 Manuel Bartlett, Mexico's former secretary of the interior, told *Fortune* magazine, "At this moment in time, Mexico is a plutocracy."

His words illustrated a story about the country's financial oligarchs. The article noted that the bulk of their wealth comes from family businesses that are monopolies. They have exclusive rights in the sale or service of goods such as telephones, cement, television, and the media.

One "big business" oligarch in Mexico is Carlos Slim Helú, a self-made billionaire. As of 2012 he ranked as the world's richest person, according to *Forbes*. Slim made his fortune with Telmex, which claims 95 percent of the domestic fixed-line telecommunications business in Mexico. Slim and fellow oligarch Emilio Azcárraga, whose family owns the media giant Televisa, have considerable political authority in Mexico. This influence was evident in 2006. When Slim promoted a political reform program for Mexico, he was able to get presidential candidates and state governors to sign on.

Some people criticize the Mexican government for allowing business monopolies to thrive, saying the government should ensure that smaller companies have a fair chance to compete. According to longtime Mexican politician Manuel Camacho Solís, that would be hard to do. "The solution is not going to war [with big business], because then we would provoke chaos in the country," Solís said. "But we need to recover the capacity for independent regulation, which isn't submitted to special interests."

One Mexican senator worried about the power of Televisa. It has four billionaires sitting on its board. "The board of Televisa [reaches] many dimensions of the economic and political life of the country," the senator noted. "It has the power to impose its own agenda on the constitutional powers of the country."

RUSSIAN OLIGARCHS

For most of the 20th century Russia was part of the Union of Soviet Socialist Republics, also known as the Soviet Union. Headed by the elites of the Communist Party, the government claimed to follow the principles of communism, in which all productive property is owned by the state.

After the Soviet Union broke apart in 1991, Russia became an independent republic. The first freely elected president of the Russian

Federation was Boris Yeltsin (1931–2007). Yeltsin wanted to sweep away communism and promote democracy and free market capitalism. In free market capitalism, prices, production, and distribution of goods are determined by competition.

Russia's new president developed an inner circle of businessmen and entrepreneurs. Dubbed the Russian oligarchs, they were business tycoons who made investments in companies and generated jobs. In return they frequently received lucrative contracts, tax breaks, and subsidies from the Russian government. In 1995 Yeltsin privatized state-owned companies. As privileged insiders, the oligarchs had access to buy Russia's petroleum, natural gas, and

Mikhail Khodorkovsky, former owner of Russian oil giant Yukos, is pictured behind bars during his 2004 trial for fraud and tax evasion in Moscow. The former oligarch has become a hero to some Russians for standing up to Vladimir Putin, who has been criticized as an autocratic ruler.

metals companies at bargain prices. Many people saw this as "crony capitalism." Such practices would be illegal in many countries, but at the time no laws were in place in Russia to make them illegal.

As the tycoons grew richer, most of the rest of Russia's citizens grew poorer. They blamed their poverty and the country's rampant inflation on Russia's fledgling democracy and the system of capitalism. Few of the poor admired the oligarchs, who were seen as having come to power at the expense of everyone else.

In December 1999 Yeltsin announced his resignation. He appointed his aide Vladimir Putin—a former agent in the KGB, the Soviet Union's national security agency—as acting president. After winning the presidential election the following March, Putin set about consolidating power. And he told Russia's oligarchs they were to stay out of politics. Oil magnate Mikhail Khodorkovsky ignored the warning and continued to fund opposition parties. In October 2003 he was arrested and jailed. His arrest reflected the waning influence of the Russian oligarchs on government policy under Putin.

Boris Berezovsky was another politically active oligarch who lost power after Putin's election. In the 2000 elections, Berezovsky supported Putin. He even used his ownership of Russia's major television channel, ORT, to discredit Putin's opponent. Berezovsky was elected to the Duma, Russia's legislative body. But soon after, he resigned from office. He began criticizing Putin's government. When Russian officials called on him to

appear for questioning, he was abroad. Berezovsky did not return to Russia. He remains in exile.

Critics of Putin accuse him of re-creating an authoritarian state in Russia. Some analysts say that he also created a new oligarchy.

Putin is close to a small group of KBG veterans. These men now make strategic decisions in government. And through their political clout, they hold positions such as deputy head of presidential administration, head of Russia's federal

Exiled former Russian oligarch Boris Berezovsky attends a political protest in front of the Russian Embassy in London, August 2010.

security service (FSB), and first deputy prime minister. Some of them have also reaped financial rewards.

The Russian oligarchs who followed Putin's advice to stay out of politics have continued to be successful. In 2008, one survey showed that Russia had 101 billionaires—the most in the world.

AMERICA'S ROBBER BARONS

During the 19th century, in a time now known as "the Gilded Age," the United States had a few financial oligarchs. Men like oil baron John D. Rockefeller, steel industrialist Andrew Carnegie, and financier J. P. Morgan amassed great fortunes. They, along with a handful of other industrial magnates who ruthlessly acquired their wealth, were known as robber barons. As oligarchs, they also had great political power.

During the so-called Panic of 1907, an economic crisis drove banks and businesses into bankruptcy. The crisis threatened to cause the collapse of the U.S. economy. J. P. Morgan was crediting with ending the

During the late 19th century, the United States was expanding westward and industries were growing rapidly, enabling businessmen like the banker J. P. Morgan (left), the railroad tycoon Jay Gould (center), and the oil magnate John D. Rockefeller (right) to amass enormous fortunes. These industrialists—sometimes nicknamed "robber barons," because they had exploited American workers to gain their wealth—used their money to influence government.

> The Communist Party holds ultimate authority in China, with major policy decisions made by the Central Committee, the Politburo, and the nine-member Politburo Standing Committee. Some analysts say that the Standing Committee is an oligarchy. Communist China is essentially run by the group, which often meets in secret sessions.

panic by pledging his own funds—and convincing other wealthy bankers to do the same—to prop up the U.S. banking system.

Two decades later, in 1929, a severe failure in the banking system occurred. It led the federal government to put in place many regulations designed to prevent the country's financial institutions from taking on too much risk.

THE 2008 ECONOMIC CRISIS

Attitudes toward regulation began to shift in the 1980s, and efforts to deregulate the U.S. financial sector gained momentum under the administrations of President Bill Clinton (1993–2001) and President George W. Bush (2001–2008). Congress passed legislation that weakened government regulation of the financial industry. Provisions of the Glass-Steagall Act of 1933, a law separating commercial banking from riskier investment banking, were repealed in 1999. The Securities and Exchange Commission (SEC)—the federal agency tasked with enforcement of the financial industry—relaxed its oversight.

During the 1990s and early 2000s investment firms and hedge fund companies created complex new products. These financial products had names like mortgage-backed securities, collateralized debt obligations, and credit-default swaps. They helped people working in the financial services and banking industries make lots of money. Companies made huge profits. And their employees took home lavish bonuses.

Unfortunately, many of the financial transactions were based on faulty economics. By 2008 it became clear that the U.S. financial sector had created too much risk, and the country suffered a sudden economic crisis. To prevent an economic meltdown, the U.S. government stepped in and helped engineer bailouts for many banking and investment firms. It helped broker the sales of some businesses. And it followed up with more bailouts.

Still, the U.S. economy contracted. By 2009 there were mass layoffs. Unemployment rates rose around the country. Some economists blamed the crisis on the financial leaders who had amassed great wealth before the crisis. These new financial oligarchs not only caused the financial crisis, they said, but also used their political influence to block the reforms needed to turn the economy around.

OCCUPY WALL STREET

Three years after the bank bailouts, in 2011, hundreds of protesters in New York City voiced their anger with Wall Street. The encampment in Zuccotti Park called attention to concerns about a corrupt system in the United States. Activists repeated the charge that financial oligarchs had for years reaped huge private rewards by making risky investments but then, when those investments went bad, used their influence in the U.S. government to make the public pick up the cost.

The Occupy Wall Street protest touched a nerve with much of the public. After the Occupy movement in New York began, similar protests took place in hundreds of American cities. They included Boston, Massachusetts; Oakland, California; Washington, D.C.; and Atlanta, Georgia.

"THE NET WORTH OF THE RICHEST 500 TO 1,000 OLIGARCHS IN THE U.S. IS ABOUT 20,000 TIMES THAT OF THE AVERAGE AMERICAN HOUSEHOLD IN THE BOTTOM 90 PERCENT. THAT'S TWICE THE WEALTH CONCENTRATION OF THE SENATORS OF IMPERIAL ROME, WHO WERE ONLY 10,000 TIMES RICHER THAN THE AVERAGE SMALL FARMER OR SLAVE WHO POPULATED THE EMPIRE."

—U.S. POLITICAL SCIENTIST JEFFREY WINTERS

A protester participates in an Occupy Wall Street march in New York, May 2012. The sign she carries indicates that 99 percent of Americans are tired of abuses by the "wealthiest 1 percent"—a group that most people believe exerts an unfair amount of influence over the American political system.

POWER OF MONEY

Banking officials were not Occupy Wall Street's only targets. Of major concern were excessively rich individuals and corporations. The protesters expressed fear that political power had become concentrated in the hands of an oligarchy. A small minority of extremely wealthy people seemed to hold much greater power than the rest of the country. Their influence meant they could successfully lobby the federal government to allow extensive deregulation of their industries. Their political contacts helped them obtain subsidies, gain lucrative government contracts, and protect their firms from competitors. Their companies paid little or no taxes because they had helped put in place self-serving loopholes in the tax code.

Activists also pointed to a controversial 2010 Supreme Court decision as an example of the financial oligarchy's influence. In *Citizens United v. Federal Election Commission*, the Court ruled that corporations had the right to spend unrestricted amounts of money in election campaigns. The ruling allowed the rich to contribute as much as they wanted in political campaigns.

The decision led to the founding of groups that can essentially receive and spend unlimited amounts of money to sway the political process. Among the super-rich who have directly funded political groups are billionaire brothers David and Charles Koch, financier George Soros, hedge fund CEO Paul Singer, investor Harold Simmons, and real estate tycoon Bob Perry. In 2012 some super-rich tycoons directly financed the campaigns of Republican presidential candidates. Mutual funds magnate Foster Friess gave millions to Rick Santorum, while casino billionaire Sheldon Adelson bankrolled the campaign of Newt Gingrich.

ECONOMIC INEQUALITY

The Occupy Wall Street movement has pointed out the increasing disparity in wealth between the very rich, or the "1 percent," of the nation and the remaining "99 percent." Political scientist Jeffrey Winters notes that "by focusing on the gap separating the 1% from 99%, the Occupy movement has hit upon the chronic problem of oligarchy and democracy in America. The power of concentrated wealth has overwhelmed and effectively disenfranchised the majority of American citizens."

However, some economists point out that the super-rich are actually in the top "0.1 percent." Unlike most other people, the 0.1 percent can usually get credit without putting any money down. They can move profits overseas, and pay lower taxes by keeping their assets in tax havens. They are today's U.S. oligarchs.

Activists have called on lawmakers to put an end to the outsized influence that the super-rich have on the U.S. government. One new step that is needed, activists say, is to put a cap on the amount of money donated in political elections. They call for legislation that will provide transparency in government, such as requiring that the identities of political donors be revealed.

OLIGARCHY AND DEMOCRACY

As elected leaders, oligarchs have been a part of democracies and republics. As advisers to monarchs, dictators, and presidents, oligarchs have wielded power behind the throne.

Throughout history oligarchies have exerted economic and political pressure to shape public policies and government actions. But the past—and the present—has also shown that oligarchic rule often leads to civil unrest.

CHAPTER NOTES

p. 9:   "Great then is the . . ." Aristotle, quoted in Benjamin Jowett, trans., *Politics*, Book IV, Part XI. http://www.constitution.org/ari/polit_04.htm

p. 9:   "[W]here the middle class . . ." Ibid.

p. 9:   "Democrats say that justice . . ." Aristotle, quoted in Jowett, *Politics, Book VI, Part III.* http://www.constitution.org/ari/polit_06.htm

p. 11:   "Who says organization . . ." Robert Michels, *Political Parties: A Sociological Study of the Oligarchical Tendencies of Modern Democracy* (New York: Hearst's International Library, 1915), p. 401.

p. 11:   "The common thread . . ." Jeffrey A. Winters, *Oligarchy* (New York: Cambridge University Press, 2011), p. 276.

p. 12:   "To argue that the United States . . ." Jeffrey A. Winters, "Oligarchy in the U.S.A.," *In These Times* (February 27, 2012). http://www.inthesetimes.com/article/12698/oligarchy_in_the_u.s.a/

p. 16:   "In all ages, whatever . . ." Ronald Syme, *The Roman Revolution* (Oxford, England: Oxford University Press, 1939), p. 7.

p. 27:   "In the case of occupied . . ." Niccolò Machiavelli, quoted in Rufus Goodwin, trans., *The Prince* (Boston: Dante University Press, 2003), p. 44.

p. 45:   "rancid oligarchy," Hugo Chavez, quoted in Sibylla Brodzinsky, "Leftwing Dictator or Saviour of the Poor: Chávez Faces New Challenge to his Rule," *Guardian*, May 24, 2004. http://www.guardian.co.uk/world/2004/may/25/venezuela.sibyllabrodzinsky

p. 47:   "From Colombia, Venezuela . . ." Matthew Walter, "Chavez Says Colombian 'Oligarchs' Threaten Venezuela," *Bloomberg*, February 4, 2008. http://www.bloomberg.com/apps/news?pid=newsarchive&sid=abo41Z9ntHLQ

p. 48:   "At this moment . . ." Feike De Jong, "And the Winner Is . . .: Whatever the Outcome of Mexico's Elections, the Oligarchs Are Likely to Come Out on Top," *Fortune*, July 10, 2006. http://money.cnn.com/magazines/fortune/fortune_archive/2006/07/10/8380923/index.htm

p. 48:   "The solution is not . . ." Ibid.

p. 48:   "The board of Televisa . . ." Ibid.

p. 53:   "The net worth . . ." Jeffrey Winters, "Romney a Nobody Among the Ultra-Wealthy, But Rich Enough to Stick Out as President," *Huffington Post*, January 12, 2012. http://www.huffingtonpost.com/jeffrey-winters/romney-a-nobody-among-the_b_1202679.html

p. 55:   "by focusing on . . ." Jeffrey Winters, quoted in "New Book Chronicles 'Oligarchy,'" Institute for Public Accuracy, October 19, 2011. http://www.accuracy.org/release/new-book-chronicles-oligarchy-2/

CHRONOLOGY

8TH–6TH CENTURY BC: Oligarchies are established in many city-states in Greece.

509 BC: The Roman Republic is established. It is run by the oligarchic Senate.

4TH CENTURY BC: The Greek philosopher Aristotle describes oligarchy as a form of government.

27 BC: Ongoing conflict between the Senate oligarchy and plebeians helps lead to the fall of the Roman Republic and the establishment of the Roman Empire.

CA. 1300–1494:   Powerful oligarchies rule city-states in northern and central Italy.

1581:   The Dutch Republic, in which merchant oligarchies rule cities and provinces, is founded.

1500s–1800s: The Spanish and Portuguese establish colonies in Central and South America that give rise to oligarchies of white European elites.

1948–1994:   The government policy of apartheid in South Africa results in oligarchic rule by whites.

1995:   During the administration of President Boris Yeltsin, Russian oligarchs make use of insider status to buy the majority of Russia's state assets.

2011:   In September the first Occupy Wall Street protests against financial oligarchy take place in New York City.

2012:   The U.S. presidential election is the most expensive in history, with the candidates of the Republican and Democratic parties raising over $500 million. So-called SuperPACs, mostly funded by wealthy donors, spend an additional $250 million during the presidential campaign.

GLOSSARY

ARISTOCRACY—an elite or upper class of society whose members hold hereditary titles or offices; rule by a privileged class.

AUTOCRATIC—describing a ruler with absolute power.

CAPITALISM—an economic system in which a country's trade and industry are controlled by private owners for profit, without intervention by the government.

COMMUNISM—a system in which property and goods are owned or controlled by the state.

CONFEDERATION—a political union created by treaty or constitution.

CRONY CAPITALISM—a form of corrupt capitalism in which business success results because of the close relationships between businesspeople and senior government officials.

DEMOCRACY—a system of government in which political authority is retained by the people, who exercise this authority through voting.

DESPOTISM—a government headed by a cruel or oppressive ruler holding absolute power.

ELITE—a small number of people who have significant influence over social and political change.

INDIGENOUS—native to; originating in a certain place.

MAGNATE—a wealthy or influential businessperson.

MONARCHY—a form of government headed by a king, queen, or emperor.

MONOPOLY—in business, the exclusive possession or control of the supply of a material or service.

OLIGARCH—a member of an oligarchy.

OLIGARCHY—a form of government in which a small group of people holds power, often for their own benefit.

PLUTOCRACY—a form of government in which the very wealthy rule.

REPUBLIC—a representative democracy in which representatives elected by the people—and not the people themselves—vote on legislation.

FURTHER READING

FOR OLDER READERS

Cartledge, Paul. *Ancient Greece: A History in Eleven Cities*. New York: Oxford University Press, 2010.

Johnson, Simon, and James Kwak. *13 Bankers: The Wall Street Takeover and the Next Financial Meltdown*. New York: Pantheon Books, 2010.

Mackay, Christopher S. *The Breakdown of the Roman Republic: From Oligarchy to Empire*. New York: Cambridge University Press, 2009.

Winters, Jeffrey A. *Oligarchy*. New York: Cambridge University Press, 2011.

FOR YOUNGER READERS

Ancient Greece: An Illustrated History. Tarrytown, N.Y.: Marshall Cavendish, 2011.

Editors of Time Magazine. *What Is Occupy: Inside the Global Movement*. New York: TIME Books, 2011.

Wagner, Heather Lehr. *The Medicis: A Ruling Dynasty*. New York: Chelsea House, 2005.

INTERNET RESOURCES

http://www.constitution.org/ari/polit_00.htm

This website hosted by the Constitution Society provides online access to the eight books of Aristotle's *Politics*, first translated by Benjamin Jowett in the 19th century.

http://www.pbs.org/frontlineworld/stories/moscow/billionaires.html

The website for the PBS program *Frontline/World* provides additional information on its 2003 story on Russian capitalism. The site includes background on Russia's oligarchs and their political power.

http://www.learner.org/interactives/renaissance/florence.html

This resource, hosted by Annenberg Learner, provides information on Florence during the time of the Italian Renaissance.

http://topics.nytimes.com/top/reference/timestopics/organizations/o/ occupy_wall_street/index.html

The "Times Topic: Occupy Movement (Occupy Wall Street)" provides background, commentary, and archival information about Occupy Wall Street from the *New York Times*.

INDEX

Numbers in **bold italics** refer to captions.

CONTRIBUTORS

Senior Consulting Editor **TIMOTHY J. COLTON** is Morris and Anna Feldberg Professor of Government and Russian Studies and is the chair of the Department of Government at Harvard University. His books include *The Dilemma of Reform in the Soviet Union* (1986); *Moscow: Governing the Socialist Metropolis* (1995), which was named best scholarly book in government and political science by the Association of American Publishers; *Transitional Citizens: Voters and What Influences Them in the New Russia* (2000); and *Popular Choice and Managed Democracy: The Russian Elections of 1999 and 2000* (with Michael McFaul, 2003). Dr. Colton is a member of the editorial board of World Politics and Post-Soviet Affairs.

LEEANNE GELLETLY is the author of several books for young adults, including biographies of Harriet Beecher Stowe, Mae Jemison, Roald Dahl, Ida Tarbell, and John Marshall.